D0700021

FIVE
METAPHYSICAL
PARADOXES

The Aquinas Lecture, 2006

FIVE METAPHYSICAL PARADOXES

Howard P. Kainz

MARQUETTE
UNIVERSITY

PRESS

Under the auspices of the
Wisconsin-Alpha Chapter of Phi Sigma Tau

Library of Congress Cataloging-in-Publication Data

Kainz, Howard P.
 Five metaphysical paradoxes / Howard P. Kainz.—
1st ed.
   p. cm.—(Aquinas lecture ; 2006)
  Includes bibliographical references.
  ISBN-13: 978-0-87462-173-0 (hardcover : alk.
paper)
  ISBN-10: 0-87462-173-9 (hardcover : alk. paper)
  1. Paradox. I. Title. II. Series.
BC199.P2K34 2006
165—dc22

                                        2005037915

Printed in the United States of America.

MARQUETTE UNIVERSITY PRESS
MILWAUKEE

The Association of Jesuit University Presses

Prefatory

The Wisconsin-Alpha Chapter of Phi Sigma Tau, the International Honor Society for Philosophy at Marquette University, each year invites a scholar to deliver a lecture in honor of St. Thomas Aquinas.

The 2006 Aquinas Lecture, *Five Metaphysical Paradoxes*, was delivered on Sunday, February 26, 2006, by Howard P. Kainz, Professor Emeritus from Marquette University.

Howard Kainz studied Greek, Latin, and Philosophy at the University of California and at Loyola University, Los Angeles (B.A.). After an M.A. in the History of Philosophy at St. Louis University, he finished his Ph.D. at Duquesne University, specializing in 19th Century German Philosophy. He was an Assistant Professor at Duquesne, then subsequently at Marquette, where he became full professor in 1981, and professor emeritus in 2002.

Professor Kainz has been awarded a National Endowment for the Humanities Fellowship for research in 1977-78, and two Fulbright Fellowships for study in Germany, 1981-82 and 1987-88.

Among the publications of Professor Kainz are the following books: *Natural Law: A Reevalua-*

tion (2004), *Politically Incorrect Dialogues* (1999), *G.W.F. Hegel: The Philosophical System* (1996), *An Introduction to Hegel: The Stages of Modern Philosophy* (1996), *Democracy and the 'Kingdom of God'* (1993), *Ethics in Context: Toward a Definition and Differentiation of the Morally Good* (1988), *Paradox, Dialectic and System: A Contemporary Reconstruction of the Hegelian Problematic* (1988), *Democracy East and West: A Philosophical Overview* (1984), *Ethica Dialectica: A Study of Ethical Oppositions* (1979), *Hegel's Phenomenology, Part I: Analysis and Commentary* (1976), *Hegel's Phenomenology, Part II: The Evolution of Ethical and Religious Consciousness to the Absolute Standpoint* (1983), *Active and Passive Potency in Thomistic Angelology* (1972). In addition to some sixty scholarly articles and book reviews, he has also published a translation with commentary: *Selections from Hegel's Phenomenology of Spirit: Bilingual Edition* (1994); two textbooks: *The Philosophy of Man: A New Introduction to Some Perennial Issues* (1981), *Hegel's Philosophy of Right with Marx's Commentary: A Handbook for Students* (1974); and two collections: *Philosophical Perspectives on Peace: An Anthology of Classical and Modern Sources* (1987), *The Legacy of Hegel*, with J. O'Malley, L. Rice (1973).

To Professor Kainz's distinguished list of publications, Phi Sigma Tau is pleased to add: *Five Metaphysical Paradoxes.*

Table of Contents

Director's notes:

The image on page 14 is printed by license © from the Corbis Corporation. The full title is *Woodcut of a Man Exploring the Meeting of the Earth and the Sky* from *Popular Astronomy* by Camille Flammarion. You can see a color image (click on it to make it larger) online by searching for image # SB001406 at the Corbis web site: http://pro.corbis.com/

The image on page 21 is from an article by Professor Seámus Davis in *Nature* 403, 746 (2000). The article is available @ http://www.nature.com/nature/journal/v403/n6771/index.html. Further, for a color image, see J.C. Davis Group, Laboratory of Atomic and Solid State Physics, Cornell University @ this web site:

http://people.ccmr.cornell.edu/~jcdavis/stm/results/zinc/

Preface

Father Roland Teske of Marquette gave his 1996 Aquinas Lecture on the topic, "Paradoxes of Time in Saint Augustine." This was the first Aquinas Lecture concerned with paradoxes, and mine is the second. Whether we have started any important precedents is doubtful. If this practice were to continue, I would consider this development paradoxical, in at least one of the senses of that word. But there are other senses; and this motivates me to offer some initial definitions:

In the *Oxford English Dictionary*, the first meaning of "paradox" is given as "a statement or tenet contrary to received opinion or belief." But this is paradox in the widest possible sense—similar to the way we use and overuse the word, "oxymoron," to indicate things or states of affairs that we simply consider contradictory. For example, a Democrat might say that "compassionate conservative" is an oxymoron, a Republican might say the same thing about a "pro-life liberal"—in both cases with the meaning that such phrases are obviously self-contradictory. But strictly speaking, an oxymoron is something that sounds contradictory but is true—as, for example, the familiar literary expressions, "a deafening silence," "living death," "lonely crowd," or the descriptions by

Shakespeare's Romeo of romantic passion as "cold fire," "feather of lead" and "sick health."

Similar ambiguities of meaning take place with the word, "paradox": David Shaw points out that the word, "paradox," is itself paradoxical, since it can mean *either* something that sounds false, but is really true, *or* something that sounds true, but is really false.[1] Personally, I find it hard to think of examples of the second type that Shaw mentions—statements that seem true but are really false. I did some research in the *World Book Encyclopedia Dictionary*, and found a statement by Oliver Wendell Holmes that might fit that definition: Holmes speaks of the "glorious epicurean paradox...: 'give us the luxuries of life, and we will dispense with its necessaries." I think you will admit that that has to be false, although it may sound true. Or maybe the statement by Luis Buñel: "I'm still an atheist, thank God!"

In any case, I am not speaking here of paradoxes in that sense, but in the first sense—statements that seem false, but are true. And I will focus specifically on the sphere of metaphysics, where some important and insufficiently noted paradoxes have lingered for some time.

But before beginning, I might mention some autobiographical factors that led to my interest

---

1 W. David Shaw, *Elegy & Paradox: Testing the Conventions* (Baltimore: John Hopkins University Press, 1994), p. 2.

in paradox. During the sixties I was a graduate student finishing up my studies for a doctorate in philosophy, and ideas began to occur to me that are perhaps the closest approximations I have had to intellectual inspirations: I began to think of various paradoxes in politics, religion, and ethics—often related to the news of the day, or to things I was reading at the time. I duly jotted down some of these ideas, and for the most part they are residing on yellowed sheets of paper in the "back burner" sections of my cabinets. Some of the ideas are obscure even to me—I can't remember what I was thinking or responding to at the time. But as this continued, I "put two and two together" and began to suspect why I was getting these ideas. The culprit was the German philosopher, G.W.F. Hegel. It just so happened that I was working on my dissertation on Hegel's *Phenomenology* at the time, and Hegelian dialectic was my daily reading matter. Well, the inspirations finally subsided, but my suspicions of the Hegelian connection remained. During the eighties, I finally worked out some connections of dialectic with paradox to my satisfaction, and published a book detailing the conclusions I had come to.[2] Towards the end of this book, I even made the timid suggestion that paradox may be the

2 Howard Kainz, *Paradox, Dialectic and System: A Contemporary Reconstruction of the Hegelian Problematic* (University Park: Pennsylvania State University Press, 1988).

most appropriate form for presenting philosophical truths in general; and I was pleased, but also a little surprised, that none of the reviewers of this book took exception to that suggestion. Perhaps they didn't read it all the way to the end. In any case, the following sections will indicate the sort of thing I have in mind, for expressing philosophical truths as bona fide paradoxes.

Paradox in the Macrocosm

Immanuel Kant in the Second Edition of his *Critique of Pure Reason* (1787) develops what he calls the four "antinomies of pure reason."[3] Each of these antinomies[4] has to do with problems that Kant considered to be perennial issues in meta-physics, but transcending all possible experience, and thus insoluble. To illustrate the insolubility of each issue, Kant shows that contradictory conclusions can be drawn in each case. He thus puts each antinomy in "thesis-antithesis" form. The thesis of each antinomy is defended by a rational approach, involving conceptual analysis. The antithesis is then defended by an empirical examination.

---

3 Norman Kemp Smith translation (New York: St. Martin's Press, 1965), A426=B454.

4 *Merriam Webster's Collegiate Dictionary* defines "antinomy" as "a contradiction between two apparently equally valid principles or between inferences correctly drawn from such principles."

Kant's first antinomy concerns the "big picture," the macrocosm, and considers a question frequently discussed by philosophers and scientists—whether the universe is finite or infinite. The "thesis" of the first antinomy is that the world a) has a beginning in time, and b) in regard to space is also enclosed in boundaries. The "antithesis" of the first antinomy is that the world has no beginning, and no limits in space, but is, in relation both to time and space, infinite. The thesis of the first antinomy—the finitude of time and space—is defended by showing that infinite time would lead to a ridiculous conclusion (*reductio ad absurdum*). Kant argues a) if time were really infinite, there would not only be an infinity of past events, but an infinity in the other direction; time would not come to a halt in the present. And b) if there were an infinite space, we would have to conceptualize all the various parts of space being enumerated in an infinite time—but he has just shown infinite time to be impossible.

But then Kant goes on to defend the antithesis, that time and space are indeed infinite. He defends this by a recourse to our experience of beginnings, which always imply preexisting successions and not a void; and our experience of extended objects which always are accompanied by other extended objects, and never lead into a void. This argument brings to my mind and imagination a medieval woodcut which you may have seen. In this woodcut, by an anonymous artist, a peasant is depicted at the edge of the universe, peering out into the empyrean heaven, beyond all space. But Kant is saying, of course, that there can't be any edge where space ends, because every edge leads into more space.

More recent, updated versions of this antinomy regarding "finite vs. infinite universe" have been found throughout a great part of the 20th century, in the debates between proponents of the BigBang theory (originally called the "primeval atom theory") and the Steady State theory. The "Steady State" theory was still popular into the 1960s. As a grad student then, I took a course on Aristotle's physics, which theorized about an eternal universe,

At the edge of the universe.

with the earth being in the middle of about 57 heavenly spheres. I decided to read some books by contemporary scientists, to get a scientific update, as much as a philosophy grad student, steeped in Thomism, could muster. I chose books by Fred Hoyle, Hermann Bondi, and Georges Lemaître.[5] Hoyle favored the "Steady State" theory, and this was still considered a viable theory at that time, the early 60s. According to Hoyle, new matter was being continually created to replenish a continually expanding universe. I kept thinking how strange it was for a self-proclaimed atheist to hold to continual creation, presumably out of nothing. But Hoyle's theory seemed to be something like a scientific update on the theory of Aristotle that I was studying in class, which also supposed that the world was eternal and unchanging.

Lemaître's theory of the "primaeval atom," on the other hand, stood in sharp contrast with the Steady State theory. And it just so happened that at that time, when I was reading about the contest between these two competing theories, Lemaître's approach gained the upper hand. This was in 1965, when the radiation belt emanating from the Big Bang was discovered. In the space of a few years, even

5 Fred Hoyle, *The Nature of the Universe* (New York: Harper, 1950); Hermann Bondi, *Cosmology* (Cambridge: Cambridge University Press, 1952); Georges Lemaître, *L'Hypothèse de l'atom primitif* (Paris: Dunoid, 1946).

the most adamant steady-state theorists began to
accept the Big Bang theory. Fred Hoyle, who had
sarcastically created the term, "Big Bang," stood fast
in his opposition to the newly verified theory; but
also found evidence for "fine tuning" in the origin
of organic compounds in the universe that caused
his "faith in atheism" to be shaken![6]

In short, physics seems to have overcome Kant's
antinomy, at least in terms of our own universe.
Scientists, whether atheists or theists or agnostics,
speak now about the Big Bang as a "singularity," a
term which avoids specifics of just what happened
"way back when." Of course, to say the universe
began with a "singularity" is not very satisfying to
the human mind, which has a bad habit of tracing
things back to their causes. To avoid this embarrassment, some theorists have speculated about
a "mother universe" that gave birth to our "baby"
universe, or about an infinite number of universes
which just by chance resulted in one universe able
to support life, or to "parallel universes" into whose
dimensions we might enter if we had some "cutting

---

6 Fred Hoyle, "The Universe: Past and Present
  Reflections," *Engineering & Science*, November 1981,
  p. 12: "A common sense interpretation of the facts sug-
  gests that a superintellect has monkeyed with physics,
  as well as with chemistry and biology, and that there
  are no blind forces worth speaking about in nature.
  The numbers one calculates from the facts seem to
  me so overwhelming as to put this conclusion almost
  beyond question."

edge" *Star Trek* paraphanalia. It is very interesting to see such a myriad of theories. Once upon a time, metaphysicians were roundly criticized for wild speculations; but now it seems that scientists in white coats are taking up the speculative mantle. But they are not getting a complete *carte blanche*. The physicist, Paul Davies, for example, notes that such theories are getting far beyond the "ground rules" for science. They are unscientific, because they are unfalsifiable. No evidence could conceivably be provided to anyone who doubts that there are multiple universes, and asks for proof.[7]

On the other hand, one can sympathize with those who want to avoid talking about any absolute beginning, for the idea is absolutely paradoxical. St. Augustine realized this. In Augustine's day, a joke was making the rounds: "What was God doing before the creation of the world? The answer: Preparing hell for people who ask questions like that."[8] Augustine in Book XI of his *Confessions* said that he wanted to go beyond such flippant answers.

7 Paul Davies, *The Mind of God: The Scientific Basis for a Rational World* (New York: Touchstone/Simon & Schuster, 1992), p. 190.

8 The source of this joke/conundrum, according to Roland Teske, in his discussion of the first of three time-paradoxes in the 1996 Aquinas Lecture, was the Manichaean cosmology, involving the conflict between subsistent good and evil principles. Augustine, originally a follower of Manichaeism, was finally able to rise above his cosmological impasses under the influence of

And after some impassioned searching, in this and
other works, he offers his formulation of the paradox: The world was created simultaneously with
time, and there was no time until the world was
created.[9] Note that in the preceding sentence, following Augustine, I have used the words, "simultaneously" and "until"—admittedly inaccurate terms
that are used merely because of a lack of better ones.
And this terminological difficulty helps bring out
the paradox: If, as all signs seem to indicate, the
world is what Kant would call a "finite" world, its
beginning would not be a temporal beginning in
any meaningful sense. It's *a beginning that is not a*

Plotinus' philosophy concerning the unity and eternity
of the divine nature.

9 Cf. *Confessions*, Edward B. Pusey trans. (Chicago:
Encyclopedia Brittanica, 1952), XI:40: "Men...say,
'What did God do before He made heaven and
earth?' ... Let them see...that time cannot be without
created being, and cease to speak that vanity." See
also Augustine's *City of God*, Marcus Dods trans.
(Chicago: Encyclopedia Brittanica, 1952), XI, 6: "If
God had made anything before the rest, this thing
would rather be said to have been made "in the beginning," — then assuredly the world was made, not in
time, but simultaneously with time. For that which
is made in time is made both after and before some
time, — after that which is past, before that which is
future. But none could then be past, for there was no
creature by whose movements its duration could be
measured. But simultaneously with time the world
was made, if in the world's creation change and motion
were created."

beginning. So perhaps the cosmologists are justified in calling it a "singularity" in the sense of something absolutely unique and inexpressible—or in looking for some "mother world(s)" to avoid having to use the "B-word." And the inevitable response to Kant's first antinomy would be that the universe is *neither* finite *nor* infinite in space and time, if "finite" implies a beginning, and if "infinite" implies an endless temporal process.

Paradox in the Microcosm

Kant's Second Antinomy[10] supplies the springboard to our second paradox. This antinomy has to do with whether or not there are some ultimate particles, out of which all matter is composed. The "thesis" of this antinomy uses a conceptual analysis to show the absurdity of the infinitely small—which would amount to *nothing*—and thus to argue that there must be some ultimate particles, or "atoms." But the "antithesis" argues from our common experience that any simple thing in space can be further divided, and the divided parts can be further divided, and so on. Just as in the First Antinomy, Kant considers this question undecidable, and concludes that it would be a waste of time for metaphysicians or anyone to give it any further consideration.

---

10 *Critique of Pure Reason*, A434=B464.

Kant was apparently not satisfied with Leibniz'
solution. Gottfried Leibniz, a half-century before,
had hypothesized that yes, there must be some
ultimate "simple substances," called "monads," and
no, these would not be further divisible because
they would be the absolutely simple and unextended
components of all matter.[11] Kant brings out his
main objection to Leibniz' approach in his expan-
sion of the argument of the Thesis. He considers
the Leibnizian hypothesis invalid, because an *absolutely simple* substance could not be an element of a
composite, but would be something like a self-con-
sciousness. He concludes that Leibniz is confusing
"monad" with "atom."[12]

Leibniz, almost as if responding to Kant from
the grave, goes on: "Now, where there are no con-
stituent parts there is possible neither extension,
nor form, nor divisibility. These Monads are the
true Atoms of nature, and, in fact, the Elements of
things...."[13] In other words, the ultimate constitu-
ents of composites are indivisible, because they are
unextended and, for all practical purposes, immaterial. The whole material world is composed of little

---

11 Gottfried Wilhelm Leibniz, *Monadology*, Robert
   Latta transl. (Irvine, CA: World Library Electronic
   Texts, 1994), Init.: "There must be simple substances
   because there are composites; for a composite is nothing else than a collection of simple substances."

12 *Critique of Pure Reason*, A442=B470.

13 *Monadology*, ibid.

immaterial points. Leibniz also theorizes that the monads have various degrees of consciousness. So, "conscious points of light or energy" might be a close approximation to Leibniz' idea.

One of my favorite books on science is by the experimental physicist and Nobel Prizelaureate, Leon Lederman.[14] Lederman has a great sense of humor to match his intriguing explanations of what goes on in particle-accelerator laboratories like Fermilab, in Batavia, Illinois, where he was formerly the director. Lederman tells us that pictures of atoms have been taken with "scanning tunneling microscopes"—so that atoms are no longer just hypothesized, but actually seen, with the proper instruments.[15] But what are now called "atoms" are not the ultimate particles; we know that the atom has multiple components. So Kant's question about whether there are any *really* ultimate particles is still relevant.

Image of the electronic wavefunction caused by scattering of electrons off a zinc atom

14 Leon Lederman with Dick Teresi, *The God Particle: If the Universe Is the Answer, What Is the Question?* (New York: Bantam Doubleday, 1994), p. 14. See ibid., p. 191.
15 See *The God Particle*, p. 191.

The equivalent in contemporary physics to Leibnizian monads would be "quarks." The inventor of quark theory, Dr. Murray Gell-Mann came up with the name "quark" from the novel *Finnegan's Wake*, by James Joyce.[16] Gell-Mann originally described quarks as merely mathematical entities. When he was asked about his reasons for this later on, he replied that he "didn't want to get into an argument with philosophers, who are an unbelievable pain in the neck, many of them saying, 'What? Real? But it can't come out! [They can't be isolated.] What do you mean saying it's real!'" But in a later interview,[17] Murray Gell-Mann clarified that quarks are real entities, not just mathematical constructs.

The existence of quarks was finally proven in 1990, and on March 2, 1995, Fermilab announced the experimental verification of the "top quark," the last of the six predicted quarks. Leon Lederman, referring to the etymology of "atom" from the Greek, *átomos*, "non-divisible," describes quarks as the *real*

---

16 In *Finnigan's Wake*, the barkeeper, H.C. Earwicker frequently says: "Three quarks for Muster Mark." Since there are three quarks in each baryon, and Gell-Mann found out about baryons first, he thought this would be an apt name—which may illustrate the importance of the humanities for bringing about new scientific developments.

17 In *Scientific American*, Mar. 1992, pp. 30-32.

"a-tom." They are "pointlike, dimensionless" and have "no real size."[18] Shades of Leibniz!

The physicists themselves lead us to various paradoxes regarding the microcosm. They tell us that particles such as photons of light are just as much waves as particles. And the physicist Fritjof Capra, in his summary of the microcosmic world, speaks about "seamless garments of interwoven events" combining all sorts of opposites.

> At the subatomic level... particles are both destructible and indestructible;...matter is both continuous and discontinuous, and force and matter are but different aspects of the same phenomenon.[19]

In this way Capra and many other quantum physicists emphasize the indeterminacy of the results

---

18 See Lederman, *The God Particle*, p. 55. Lederman's quest for many years has been to figure out why it is that quarks have mass. Lederman suspects that the Higgs field is somehow responsible for giving the particles mass, or making it appear as if they have mass. But this is a mystery, and he sees this as a major quest in contemporary particle physics—to find the "God particle," the Higgs bison. Lederman's God-particle seems to me to be comparable to the special type of monad hypothesized by Leibniz, the *soul-monad*, which would have a certain preeminence in the hierarchy of monads.

19 Fritjof Capra, *The Tao of Physics*, 3rd ed. (Boston: Shambhala, 1991), p. 149.

arrived at in their investigations, and these results do indeed seem paradoxical. But as physicist-theologian Stanley Jaki observes,[20] the fact that oppositions such as particle vs. wave, force-field vs. matter, etc. seem to be mutually convertible according to the instrumentation of the quantum physicist, does not necessarily imply that reality itself is similarly "indeterminate." The fact that we do not know whether phenomena being considered are particles or waves, etc., does not necessarily imply that particles are actually changing into waves and vice versa on the first-order level.

In any case, all current evidence indicates that the *real* paradox in the microcosm has to do with the *real* a-toms, quarks, which Lederman describes as "pointless" and "dimensionless." Here we are confronted with *ultimate particles which are not particles* in any traditionally accepted meaning. And if the strange mass of these dimensionless points is supplied by the Higgs Boson, as Lederman suspects, the quarks would be not only unextended but massless. In other words, the answer to Kant's "insoluble" antinomy seems to be that yes, there are some ultimate components of matter, but they are not material in any of the usual senses of "material"—which would imply extension and mass. So

---

20 Stanley Jaki, *The Bible and Science* (Front Royal, VA: Christendom Press, 1996), p. 150.

perhaps Leibniz was on to something important with his theory of the monads, after all.

Paradox in the Human Psyche:
Consciousness & the Unconscious

Along with the evolution of other things, the concept of "the unconscious" has evolved considerably in the last few centuries. According to Lancelot Law Whyte, the term, "unconscious," used as a noun, first appears in references to *Bewusstsein* by the German physician and philosopher, Ernst Platner, in his *Philosophische Aphorismen* (1776). Platner concentrates on a person's individual unconscious, manifested by impressions emerging from the depth of one's psyche.[21]

But in the 19th century, through the intervention of some influential German philosophers, the world's attention began to focus primarily on the unconscious in a global sense, transcending the individual (Unconscious with a capital "U"). Thus, towards the beginning of the 19th century, G.W.F. Hegel (1770-1831) speaks about the emer-

---

21 Whyte cites one of Platner's aphorisms: "Apperceptions [conscious ideas] alternate with perceptions [ideas without consciousness] throughout life—wakefulness and sleep, consciousness and unconsciousness." Lancelot Law Whyte, *The Unconscious before Freud* (New York: Basic Books, 1960), p. 116.

gence of unconscious aspects of Spirit in the social matrix, using the imagery of ancient Greek and Roman mythology. In Hegel's phenomenological construal, the "Unconscious" [*das Unbewusst*] is the raw "divine" power of Nature, personified in the gods of the underworld and in the Roman Penates (guardian spirits of families), and giving rise to paradigmatic individuals like Oedipus, Antigone, and Orestes. The antipode to these global "netherworld" unconscious forces is the global consciousness of the "upper world" polity, imposing its will on paradigmatic individuals, through certain self-proclaimed champions of the universal, such as Sophocles' character, King Creon.[22] The global conflict of consciousness encountering unconscious forces then becomes reflected in world-historical individuals like Oedipus and Antigone, who spearhead the further emergence of Spirit.[23]

Arthur Schopenhauer (1788-1860) in his *The World as Will and Idea* takes this concept of a global unconscious even further than Hegel. Schopenhauer speaks about "Will" with a capital "W" as a massive unconscious natural force expressing itself in a multiplicity of manifestations, and especially in the human will-to-life. It is interesting, however,

---

22 See *Hegel's Phenomenology of Spirit: Selections Translated and Annotated by Howard P. Kainz* (University Park, PA: Pennsylvania State University Press, 1994), §467, §473, §476.

23 See especially idem, §469, §472.

that, while Hegel in a couple places uses the noun, "*das Unbewußte*," "the Unconscious," to indicate an abstract area outside of individual or social consciousness, Schopenhauer uses "unconscious" always adjectivally, as an inseparable characteristic of the Will. According to Schopenhauer, Will, either as a universal impetus to life or in its individual manifestations, is essentially unconscious.

But the best example of a widespread fascination with the idea of the Unconscious in the late 19th century is found in the writings of Eduard von Hartmann (1842-1906). His massive three-volume work, *The Philosophy of the Unconscious*, published in German in 1868, was translated into French in 1877 and into English in 1884, turning out to be a strange and unpredictable best-seller. In Von Hartmann's formulation, "the Unconscious" is definitely used as a concrete substantive, the global unconscious force of Will, giving rise to all worldly developments. I say that the popularity of his book is "strange" in view of his theory that mankind is progressing unconsciously to something that looks very much like mass suicide! He prophecies a final state of misfortune and misery that will result in a concerted final negation of "the will to live," thus bringing about the end of the world.[24] Von

---

24 Eduard von Hartmann, *Philosophy of the Unconscious*, William Coupland trans. (New York: Harcourt, Brace and Company, 1931), Part III, pp. 135-6: "Only when the negative part of volition in humanity outweighs

Hartmann has been fittingly called the "philosopher of pessimism." Probably only a German philosopher could get away with his conclusions. It should be mentioned, however, that Von Hartmann himself denied that his projected end of the human race would be suicide in the usual sense, but rather a glorious final expression of the human Will.

But in the 20ᵗʰ century, it was Freud's theory of psychoanalysis that was most responsible for raising the notion of the unconscious to worldwide importance and attention. Freud does sometimes speak of the Unconscious with a capital "U" like his predecessors from Germany, portraying the Unconscious as an ancestral residue passed on from generation to generation. But for the most part, as is well-known, Freud is concerned with the unconscious with a small "u." He focuses on the individual unconscious, as a repository for repressed desires and memories, leading to psychic fantasies, conflicts, neuroses, and psychoses. Presiding over these unconscious well-springs, which Freud later characterized as the "Id," is a "censor" mechanism, which prevents certain inconvenient, or embarrassing, or painful contents

---

the sum of all the rest of the will objectifying itself in the organic and inorganic world, only then can the human negation of will annihilate *the whole actual volition of the world without residuum*, and cause the whole kosmos to disappear at a stroke by the withdrawal of the volition, which alone gives it existence. (That is here the only question, not as to a mere suicide of humanity *en masse*....)."

from emerging into the arena of consciousness. The skill of Freud, and Freudian psychoanalysts, using methods such as dream analysis and "talk therapy," consisted in their ability to pinpoint areas of censorship that a patient needs to recognize and deal with, in order to avoid phobias, inhibitions, neuroses, psychoses, etc.

Freud's theories were the rage from 1935-1945, and remained influential into the 50s But psychoanalysis gradually gave way to psychiatry and psychopharmacology, leading to psychologist Lee R. Steiner's 1958 prediction at Harvard University that in twenty-five years psychoanalysis "will take its place with phrenology and mesmerism.... Freud had the germ of an idea which flared into a way of life for a time, but then vanished."[25] The possible waning of psychoanalysis with the advent of psychopharmacological approaches was foreseen by Freud himself, who predicted that "in time to come it should be possible to cure hysteria [nervous diseases] by administering a chemical drug without any psychological treatment." [26]

But although Freudian psychoanalysts have become an endangered species, the notion of an

---

25 O. Hobart Mowrer, *The Crisis in Psychiatry and Religion* (Princeton: D. Van Nostrand, 1961), pp. 69f.

26 Ernest Jones, *The Life and Work of Sigmund Freud,* (New York: Basic Books, 1953), Volume 1, p. 259.

unconscious still perdures. As Ivan Soll points out,

> Freud justified the postulation of the uncon-
> scious by claiming that it helped to explain
> several sorts of otherwise incomprehensible
> human behavioral phenomena, such as para-
> praxes, dreams, memory, and various sorts of
> neurotic symptom formation.[27]

In other words, Freud's theory has other uses besides overcoming the barriers set up by an unconscious "censor." And Steiner's 1958 prediction may have been premature. Freud's theories have elicited recent surges of interest from the scientific establishment. Networks of neuroscientists and psychoanalysts have been formed throughout the world, and the journal, *Neuro-Psychoanalysis* is published by the International Neuro-Psychoanalysis Society, which holds an annual congress. Such investigators have found evidence in the nervous system supporting Freudian hypotheses regarding defense-mechanisms and mechanisms of repression, and have indicated that

> The core brain stem and limbic system—
> responsible for instincts and drives—roughly

---

27 See Ivan Soll, "Sartre's Rejection of the Freudian Unconscious," in Paul Arthur Schilpp, *Philosophy of Jean-Paul Sartre* (La Salle, IL: Open Court, 1981), p. 586.

correspond to Freud's id. The ventral frontal region, which controls selective inhibition, the dorsal frontal region, which controls self-conscious thought, and the posterior cortex, which represents the outside world, amount to the ego and the superego."[28]

But, as Mark Solms puts it, "the aspect of Freudian dream theory that is most difficult (although not impossible) to reconcile with current neuropsychological knowledge is that of censorship."[29] And misgivings about the "censor" were precisely what instigated the intense opposition to Freud on the part of the existentialist philosopher, Jean-Paul Sartre, in his *Being and Nothingness* and other works. Sartre construes the Freudian censorship mechanisms as a mere pretext, allowing patients to avoid taking responsibility for free choices they have made. Individuals who explain or excuse their actions by pointing to an unconscious censor that checks some drives, but allows others through into consciousness, are simply engaging in pure self-deception. They are caught up in what Sartre calls "bad faith"—attributing a strange "awareness-of-unconsciousness" to the censor instead of admitting their own awareness of what is going on:

28 See Mark Solms, "Freud Returns," *Scientific American*, 290:6, 82-88, at 88, May 2004.

29 Mark Solms, "Freudian Dream Theory Today," *Psychologist* 13:12, Dec. 2000, p. 618.

> The resistance of the patient implies on the
> level of the censor an awareness of the thing
> repressed as such.... But what type of self-
> consciousness can the censor have? It must be
> the consciousness (of) being conscious of the
> drive to be repressed, but precisely *in order not
> to be conscious of it*. What does this mean if not
> that the censor is in bad faith? Psychoanalysis
> has not gained anything for us since in order to
> overcome bad faith, it has established between
> the unconscious and consciousness an autono-
> mous consciousness in bad faith.[30]

In other words, the unconscious, as Sartre inter-
prets it, tries to stand as a form of knowing and not-
knowing at the same time. Sartre caricatures Freud's
"censor" as a little homunculus at the vestibule of
the unconscious, allowing certain things through
into consciousness, but blocking undesirable, alien
contents. With the help of Freudian psychoanalysts,
a patient can escape dealing with his own freedom,
and simply relegate responsibility for his actions to
this homunculus.

Sartre's discomfort with Freudian ideas can be
best understood if we take into account the fact
that he held a Cartesian concept of the transpar-

---

30 Jean-Paul Sartre, *Being and Nothingness*, Hazel Barnes
   transl. (New York: Washington Square Press, 1966),
   p. 63f.

ency of consciousness. Starting with the *cogito*[31] of René Descartes (1596-1650), Sartre focuses on an absolutely lucid type of consciousness that is "self-directed and self-contained,"[32] allowing no unassimilated opacities, no "grey areas" in choices made, no partly conditioned freedom, depending on environmental factors, etc. In short, we humans are "condemned to be free"—even if we refuse to choose, or deceive ourselves about the choices we are making. The arch-principle of ethics, according to Sartre is the manifestation of this freedom that we unquestionably have. Sartre's "ethical person" takes full responsibility for his/her actions, and avoids excuses in terms of social and environmental pressures, family background, etc.

Sartre expanded these basic principles of his theory into what is known as "existential psycho-analysis," which for some decades was a significant competitor with Freudian psychoanalysis. He gives an example of his approach, and how it differs from Freud, in the chapter on "Bad Faith" in *Being and Nothingness*. He discusses cases of women who have become sexually frigid in the aftermath of marital infidelity, as reported by the Viennese psychiatrist, Wilhelm Stekel:

---

31 Descartes' fundamental principle: *Cogito, ergo sum*: "I think, therefore I am."

32 Marjorie Grene, *Sartre* (New York: New Viewpoints, 1973), p. 121.

> Admissions which Stekel was able to draw
> out [of his patients] inform us that these
> pathologically frigid women apply themselves
> to becoming distracted in advance from the
> pleasure which they dread; many for example
> at the time of the sexual act, turn their thoughts
> away toward their daily occupations, make up
> their household accounts. Will anyone speak
> of an unconscious here?[33]

Having posed this rhetorical question, Sartre
offers what he considers to be the obvious and
unavoidable answer: "If the frigid woman thus dis-
tracts her consciousness from the pleasure which
she experiences,... *it is in order to prove to herself* that
she is frigid."[34] Sartre's diagnosis, is the diagnosis of
a bona fide existentialist psychoanalyst: Such people
are in "bad faith"; and their Freudian psychoanalysts
are simply helping them to find excuses for what
clearly amounts to self-deception.

The opposition of Sartre to Freud became a *cause
célèbre* in the mid-twentieth century, even leading
to an invitation from the Hollywood director, John
Huston, to write a screenplay, in which Marilyn
Monroe would play the part of one of Freud's
famous patients, Cäcilie. Huston offered Sartre a
handsome commission, and Sartre went to work,
producing a very long screen play which would have

33 *Being and Nothingness*, p. 65.
34 Ibid. Italics are in the original.

resulted in a seven-hour movie. Huston patiently asked for a rewrite compatible with a two-hour movie. Sartre initially agreed, but became so bored with the task that Huston finally had some of his own screenwriters work on it, resulting in *Freud: the Secret Passion*, starring Montgomery Clift as Freud, but without Marilyn Monroe.[35]

But Sartre's approach—replacing analysis of the unconscious with detection and avoidance of "bad faith"—seems to present difficulties equal in magnitude to the Freudian problems. For "bad faith" as self-deception, "lying to oneself," implies *both* knowing the truth, *and* intentionally using devices to hide the truth from oneself, thus keeping the truth from oneself—in other words, a self-contradiction—a paradox in the bad sense. Freud—to give credit where credit is due—actually avoids the contradiction entailed by Sartre's idea of self-deception, by dividing the psyche into conscious and unconscious, so that the "deception" would be simply a mechanical process helping to defend the ego from potentially disruptive processes emerging from the Id.

Some ordinary language philosophers think they have a simple solution for this paradox of self-deception: "To deceive oneself," they tell us, is in the same

---

35 See Sartre's *The Freud Scenario*, J.-B. Pontalis, ed., Quintin Hoare transl. (Chicago: University of Chicago Press, 1985). The plan to feature Marilyn Monroe was vetoed by Freud's daughter, the psychoanalyst Anna Freud.

linguistic vein as "to invite oneself" (meaning to go to a party uninvited), or "to defeat oneself" (meaning to act so incompetently or maladroitly that you offer the opportunity for someone else to defeat you in some respect).

For what it is worth, I would also offer by analogy the custom in German grammar of using reflexive verbs to express what in English would have no reflexive sense—e.g. *Die Erde bewegt sich um die Sonne* does not mean the earth moves itself but that the earth moves or is moved around the sun, and *Es findet sich immer ein Weg* does not mean that a way always finds itself, but rather that "a way can always be found." So also, could we not say that "to deceive oneself" in similar fashion may simply mean that you are unsure about your real motives, or have no clue as to whether your behavior is caused by a physical indisposition, habits, reaction to stimuli, etc.? It is clear, however, that Sartre himself means self-deception in a stronger sense.

Freud and Sartre seem to present us with a Scylla-or-Charybdis pair of alternatives: either uphold the possibility of the intentional, purposeful self-deception which Sartre characterizes as "bad faith," or avoid the contradiction implied in the idea of "lying to oneself" by the Freudian hypothesis of an unconscious reservoir of drives, which enter or are refused entry into our consciousness by a "censor" at the boundaries of the unconscious. I would suggest, rather than saying "a plague on both their houses,"

that a reconciling, two-tiered paradox might be
entertained: The first tier of the paradox is based
on the fact that Freud distinguished between the
"unconscious" and the "preconscious," the former
being outside the reach of consciousness, the lat-
ter (the object in psychoanalysis) being residues of
our instincts welling up into consciousness.[36] In
other words, *this* preconscious aspect of the unconscious is *within consciousness.* The second tier of
the paradox is that yes, we must in Sartrean fashion resist the subterfuge of blaming our actions on
some "unconscious"—whatever that is—but also go
beyond Sartre to realize that *true freedom requires
an understanding of our instinctive side,* which con-
tains the erotic and aggressive impulses that Freud
focused on, and/or other aspects of the unconscious
emphasized by other psychoanalysts[37]—in order to
utilize, or control, or redirect, or sublimate them,

---

36 The "System Ucs." in Freudian terminology is a basi-
cally irrational complexus of desires and instincts,
and the "Pcs." (Preconscious) is the repository of
elements repressed by the "censor," which can cause
neuroses, and are recognized by the psychoanalyst if
he gets close to the resistances, through talk therapy,
free associations, etc. (It should be noted that Freud
in early works also used the term, "subconscious," but
did not employ this terminology after 1895.)

37 E.g., the drive for power that Alfred Adler, Freud's
erstwhile disciple, focused on, or the drive for self-
integration that Carl Jung, another ex-Freudian
prioritized.

with or without the assistance of a therapist. To try to "raise ourselves by our bootstraps" while ignoring or denying input and energy from our raw psychic powers would be a mistake, and no boon to personal freedom.

The Paradox of Nature & the Supernatural

I would like to start with the famous statement of David Hume (1711-1776) regarding miracles. In his treatise on *Human Understanding*, Hume writes:

> A miracle is a violation of the laws of nature; and as a firm and unalterable experience has established these laws, the proof against a miracle, from the very nature of the fact, is as entire as any argument from experience can possibly be imagined.[38]

This has been called an "a priori proof" against the possibility of miracles, since the conclusion is not derived from experience or possible experiences, but rather from a rational principle considered irrefutable and almost axiomatic. Hume's basic principle here is that if there is any real, bona fide "law of

---

38 Hume, *An Enquiry Concerning Human Understanding*, L.A. Selby-Bigge, ed. (Oxford: Clarendon Press, 1961), Sect. X, §90.

nature," it can't be violated. A law is a law is a law. The examples he gives include the laws of human mortality, laws of combustion, and the law of gravity. We might prefer to call these "laws" theories or hypotheses, since a law in the strict sense is something enacted by some duly authorized lawgiver. But scientists do refer to some extremely well-founded theories as "laws" because they show regularities and stabilities analogous to the human rational directives we call "laws."

What stands out, in Hume's argument, is his extraordinary confidence in the inviolability of the "laws of nature"—more confidence than most contemporary scientists display, who emphasize the fact that even theories which have been promoted to the status of "laws" are, in principle, falsifiable. From our privileged viewpoint of the twenty-first century, we know that some theories which had been promoted to the status of "laws" in the past by many scientists have been superseded or discarded. For example, the Newtonian theory/law of gravity has certainly been updated by Einstein's General Theory of Relativity; and, as mentioned above, the Steady State theory has now been effectively discarded in favor of the Big Bang theory.

But, although Hume was noted for his consistent scepticism in metaphysics and religion, he does in the segment on miracles offer a strange and seemingly paradoxical reference to faith as the ultimate miracle. He writes,

> Whoever is moved by *Faith* to assent to [an alleged miracle], is conscious of a continued miracle in his own person, which subverts all the principles of his understanding, and gives him a determination to believe what is most contrary to custom and experience.[39]

In view of Hume's inveterate and unceasing skepticism, this statement is obviously meant ironically—as a declaration that faith indeed would be the greatest miracle of all!—completely contrary to the laws of nature, and thus irrational. (Kierkegaard came across this statement from Hume[40] but apparently took it to heart in a positive and non-ironical sense.[41])

This Humean declaration *sounds* paradoxical, but it has to be understood in the context of a real paradox regarding miracles, which Hume helps to bring out:

---

39 *An Enquiry Concerning Human Understanding*, Sect. X, Part II, 101.

40 Kierkegaard read it in the writings of Johann Georg Hamman, possibly without knowing that Hume was the author. See Louis Pojman, "Christianity and Philosophy in Kierkegaard's Early Papers, *Journal of the History of Ideas* 44:1, 1983, p. 135.

41 For Kierkegaard, external miracles had little relevance to Christian faith, but faith itself was a great miracle of subjectivity performed by God. See, for example, *Fear and Trembling*, Walter Lowrie transl. (Princeton, NJ: Princeton University Press, 1974), pp. 47, 52, 77.

> No testimony is sufficient to establish a miracle,
> unless the testimony be of such a kind, that its
> falsehood would be more miraculous, than the
> fact, which it endeavours to establish.[42]

And what kind of testimony could meet such rigorous standards? Hume seems to set the criteria for credibility in the following statement:

> There is not to be found, in all history, any
> miracle attested by a sufficient number of men,
> of such unquestioned good-sense, education,
> and learning, as to secure us against all delusion
> in themselves.[43]

At first glance, this statement could be interpreted as a concession or qualification: What if there *are* cases of consistent and convincing reports of an event that appears to violate the laws of nature? But Hume sticks to his *a priori* guns, and responds that, in a case like this, it is *always* more probable that the testimony is mistaken than that the event took place.[44] This is due to the fact that human testimony is always fallible, while the laws of nature are inviolable.

About the closest that Hume comes to modifying this position is found in his *Dialogues Concerning Natural Religion*, published posthumously in 1779.

---

42 Ibid., X, Part I, 91.
43 Ibid., X, Part II, 92.
44 Ibid., X, Part II, 98.

In this dialogue, Cleanthes, defending religion, poses a question to Philo, who seems for the most part to represent Hume's position:

> Suppose ... that an articulate voice were heard in the clouds, much louder and more melodious than any which human art could ever reach: suppose, that this voice were extended in the same instant over all nations, and spoke to each nation in its own language and dialect: suppose, that the words delivered not only contain a just sense and meaning, but convey some instruction altogether worthy of a benevolent Being, superior to mankind.[45]

Hume, as narrator, describing the reaction of Philo to this question, writes, "Here I could observe... that Philo was a little embarrassed and confounded." But at that point in the dialogue, another character, Demea, rescues Philo (and Hume) by breaking in and raising the discussion to a mystical/fideistic level.[46]

Hume's general challenge, regarding the credibility of any human testimony about an allegedly miraculous event, has been taken up as a battle-cry by skeptics for the last few centuries. Champions of the inviolability of the "laws of nature" have shown almost a religious fervor in attacking any reports of

---

45 David Hume, *Dialogues Concerning Natural Religion* (Indianapolis: Bobbs-Merrill, 1947), Part III, p. 152.
46 Ibid., 155.

the supernatural, or even of the preternatural, that dares to raise its head. A frequent foil is the science of parapsychology, investigating ESP phenomena in universities and scientific institutes around the world, but widely criticized as a pseudo-science, in spite of apparent fidelity to accepted investigative methods in psychology. Skepticism about such investigations is encapsulated in media such as the journal, *Skeptical Inquirer*, which features articles in every issue debunking reports of evidence of telepathy, psychokinesis, and near-death experiences, as well as miracles.

But like it or not, miracles are very important for Christianity. There is a long-standing tradition in the Judaeo-Christian religious tradition of requiring "signs" as God's expression of approval for prophets and prophetical messages. Stanley Jaki, whose observation regarding the Indeterminacy Principle I referred to above, cites Pope St. Pius X's pronouncement that miracles are "most certain signs of the divine origin of the Christian religion."[47] In Christian apologetics, miracles might be compared to our present internet security requirements for electronic "signatures." The idea seems to be that a message or messenger coming from a truly supernatural source should give clear expressions of divine approval through supernatural power. In

---

47 Cf. Stanley Jaki, *Miracles and Physics* (Front Royal, VA: Christendom Press, 1989), p. 2.

the Roman Catholic tradition, lack of such expressions will lead to refusal of canonization for saints
or refusal to recognize messages from visionaries as
authentic. A recent example is the refusal of bishops
to recognize events at Medjugorje because of failure
to produce promised "signs."[48]

---

48 Bishop Pavao Zanic, ordinary of Medjugorje 1977-
   1993, interview, *Fidelity Magazine*, 13:2, February,
   1994, p. 17: "They have fabricated messages, and
   they say that you [the Virgin Mary] come and appear
   there, but beyond their own arguments they have
   nothing to prove that what they say is true. The whole
   world is in expectation of a "great sign" and the naive
   still wait and believe. Unfortunately this false sensa-
   tion will bring great disgrace and scandal upon the
   Church." Bishop Zanic's 1987 official proclamation,
   cited from Ivo Sivric, *The Hidden Side of Medjugorje*,
   Louis Belanger, ed. (Saint-Francois-du-Lac, Québec:
   Editions Psilog, 1989): "The 'sign' to me is that for six
   years you [the Blessed Virgin] steadfastly remained
   silent to all rumors about the sign: it will be, they said,
   on the hillside of apparitions, visible and permanent;
   it is going to be realized soon; it will be before long,
   in a while; be patient for a while, so they were saying
   in 1981... Then again: it will be realized on the feast
   of the Immaculate Conception, for Christmas, for the
   New Year, etc. Thank you, Madonna, because with
   your long silence of six years you have demonstrated
   that you have not spoken here, nor appeared, nor
   given any message or secret nor promised a special
   sign." Bishop Ratko Peric, Bishop Zanic's successor
   at Medjugorje from 1993 to the present, stated in
   1998: "My conviction and position is that the apparitions or revelations of Medjugorje not only *non*

Accounts of miracles do exist in non-Christian religions, but, as Kenneth Woodward, religion editor for *Newsweek* magazine, points out in his book on miracles, these accounts have a different connotation than in Christianity.[49] In the major non-Christian religions, miracles are taken as signs of spiritual power as well as compassion for others, but not as a seal of divine approval on the prophets and/or the messages.[50]

---

constat de supernaturalitate [do not give evidence of the supernatural] but *constat de non supernaturalitate* [give evidence of being non-supernatural]" (quoted from the University of Dayton International Marian Research Institute website, http://www.udayton. edu/mary/news99/0914.html).

49 Kenneth L. Woodward, *The Book of Miracles: The Meaning of the Miracle Stories in Christianity, Judaism, Buddhism, Hinduism, Islam* (New York: Simon & Schuster, 2000). Woodward defines a miracle very broadly as "an unusual or extraordinary event that is in principle perceivable by others, that finds no reasonable explanation in ordinary human abilities or in other known forces that operate in the world of time and space, and that is the result of a special act of God or the gods or of human beings transformed by efforts of their own through asceticism and meditation."

50 To summarize some of Woodward's findings: In yoga, as the ascetical/mystical offshoot of Hinduism, high states of perfection became associated with miraculous powers such as superhuman strength and the ability to levitate and traverse great distances in a moment's time. In later Judaism, Islam and Buddhism, miracles are accorded no official significance by religious lead-

But—back to Hume's nascent paradox: *A miracle should be accepted only if its rejection would be more miraculous than its acceptance.* We, especially the non-orthodox-Humeans among us, could take Hume's challenge as an open question, and simply pose the question as to whether there just might be some miracles that could satisfy even a Humean skeptic. In other words, do we have any reports of miraculous events whose falsity would be more miraculous than the events themselves?

I think the closest we have to such an event in the post-Humean world would be the reported miracle of the sun at Fatima, Portugal, in 1917. This is a miracle that was predicted by the Lady appearing to three shepherd children several months before. The children had asked the Lady for a sign, since no one believed them, and anti-clerical authorities were engaged in tactics to scare the children (even threatening to boil them in oil). On the exact day and at the exact time predicted by the apparition, the event was observed by more than 50,000 people, believers and skeptics, peasants and intellectuals, and numerous reporters, since the miracle had been predicted several times. It had been raining

---

ers. Nevertheless, in Judaism and Islam there are numerous legends of holy men curing the sick instantaneously, raising the dead, walking on water, feeding the multitudes by multiplying scarce food resources, etc. And Buddhist holy men reportedly have acquired a variety of psychic and psychokinetic powers.

all day, but at noon the children told the crowd to put down their umbrellas, and then the clouds dissipated and a series of strange gyrations of the sun began, repeated three times. The event was described by Avelina de Almeida, the editor of the liberal, Freemason, anti-clerical newspaper, *O Seculo*, as follows: "Before their dazzled eyes the sun trembled, the sun made unusual and brusque movements, defying all the laws of the cosmos, and according to the typical expression of the peasants, 'the sun danced....'"

This event, if it really took place, would be what St. Thomas Aquinas described as a "class one" miracle, the highest type in the hierarchy of miracles.[51] It certainly would seem to have met Hume's criterion, given above, regarding the presence of "men [and women] of unquestioned good-sense, education, and learning"—since those present included many university professors, atheists, anti-clerical scoffers, and reporters from various cities.

The most comprehensive examination of this event has been undertaken by the physicist and theologian, Stanley Jaki, who traveled to Portugal to interview all still-living witnesses and examine doc-

---

51 *Summa theologiae* I, q. 105, a. 8: The greatest type of miracle are things which are impossible according to nature—not just regarding the way in which it takes place, or the means by which it is done. St. Thomas gives as examples the glorification of a human body, or the retrograde movement of the sun.

umentation, eyewitness accounts, and depositions
concerning the event on Oct. 17, 1917, in Fatima,
Portugal, then published his findings in 1999.[52] Jaki
concluded that there was an overwhelming consensus, with minor variations in experiences, that
something had happened unexplainable by natural
causes.[53] Could this have been a mass hallucination?
Jaki in another book dismisses the idea that God
would resort to the creation of illusions to signify
His approval.[54] This would amount to trickery,

---

52 Stanley L. Jaki, *God and the Sun at Fatima* (Royal
   Oak, MI: Real View Books, 1999).

53 In my review of this book for *The National Catholic
   Reporter* for the April 28, 2000 issue, vol. 36 n. 26, p.
   21, I summarized Jaki's conclusions: "The prediction
   of the exact time of an event unforeseen by meteorolo-
   gists is a miracle, even if the phenomenon was natural.
   What seems to have happened is that the filmy clouds
   in front of the sun formed a massive natural "lens" (for
   which there have been precedents), with refractions
   of light causing all the colors of the rainbow. (Possibly
   the change of diameter in the lens could lead to the
   appearance of the sun getting larger and closer. Jaki
   believes that God characteristically uses natural physical developments for miracles.) His final conclusion is
   that the event at Fatima is arguably the most important
   event of the 20th century—a Providential sign for a
   century that was to witness so many incredible acts
   of inhumanity and immorality."

54 Jaki, *Bible and Science* (Front Royal, VA: Christendom
   Press, 1996), pp. 152-3: "Even for God it is not possible to let something exist and not exist at the same
   time. Therefore, in reference to his performing a

and God doesn't play tricks. Jaki also directly con-
fronts the supposition of Hume and other skeptics
that the "*necessarily* unchangeable character" of the
"laws of nature" proscribe our belief in miracles.
He comments,

> concern about the laws of nature should give
> second place to concern about man's ability to
> register things and events with certainty. And
> since without that ability nothing can be known
> about the laws of nature, the chief intellectual
> concern should be not so much about the pos-
> sible violations of the laws of nature as about
> the actual violation, if not plain rape, of man's
> mind whose natural function is to know reality
> with immediate certitude. [55]

This brings out the true paradox, with regard to
miracles and the laws of nature. Since our scientific
knowledge of the laws of nature depends, in the
last analysis, on *facts* reported by observers and
experimenters, *it would indeed be a greater miracle,
for a skeptic like Hume, to discount and discounte-
nance massive personal testimony,* than to accept that
an event took place inconsistent with the laws of
nature. Scientists themselves, if they come across

---

miracle, God cannot be assumed to force people to
believe that something took place, although it did
not. In performing his miracles God does not practice
make-believe."

55 Jaki, *Miracles and Physics*, pp. 78, 92-3.

facts which seem to contradict accepted theories, are willing to abandon or revise their theories, if the facts are corroborated. So also, reports of the miraculous, just like all the laws of nature, are based on human observations and testimony regarding observed facts; and it is the reliability of the facts that are most relevant, not the conformity or lack of conformity to scientific laws or theories.

Philology & the Limits of Language

"Philology" is an umbrella term that has gathered a number of disparate meanings over the centuries—referring either to the study of literature, or "polite learning," or comparative linguistics, or sometimes—pejoratively—as loquaciousness. Etymologically, it means "the love of words." The philosopher, Friedrich Nietzsche, as you may know, was a Professor, not of Philosophy, but of Classical Philology, in Switzerland when he wrote *The Birth of Tragedy*. I am using "philology" here in a wide sense, as including all disciplines or branches of disciplines which have to do specifically with words and the uses of words and word-formations, or the proper correspondence between words and concepts.

You may have noticed that all the metaphysical paradoxes we have examined so far in this lecture have been concerned with *boundaries*—the boundaries of the cosmos, or of the psyche, or of nature and what is "natural." In this final segment, my focus is on the boundaries of our experience with words—that is, with the limits of language.

Certainly one time-honored limit of language, and arguably the most important limit, has to do with the expression of oppositions and contradictions. Thousands of years' work in the discipline of logic have brought out the reality of that limit very well. The so-called "logical paradoxes" are thought to be a prime example of arriving at the limits of language, and a perennial bane of philosophers. It would be interesting to know how many millions of man- and woman-hours have been spent trying to dissect and explain, or avoid instantiations of, the "liar" paradox, e.g. "Every statement that I make is false," or some of the "set paradoxes" such as the question about whether the barber of Seville, who cut the hair of everyone who did not cut his or her own hair, cut his own hair. I introduced my own variation on the "set paradoxes" in the book I mentioned earlier, namely: "if a philosopher can solve paradoxes for all who cannot solve paradoxes for themselves, can he solve paradoxes for himself?" But this has not yet become famous as "Kainz's paradox."

Historically, the interest in logical paradoxes has ranged from the Megarians in ancient philosophy, to the consideration of *insolubilia* in the middle ages by John Buridan, William of Ockham, and

many others,[56] to Russell's twentieth-century work
on the set paradoxes and most recently Nicholas
Rescher's book,[57] which claims to provide the final
solution to paradoxes by systematic elimination
of "overdetermined" segments. Bertrand Russell
in his *Autobiography* reminisces about spending
whole summers staring at a blank sheet of paper
all day long, trying to come up with a solution for
set paradoxes.[58]

---

56 See e.g. G. E. Hughes, *John Buridan on Self-
Reference: Chapter Eight of Buridan's* Sophismata,
*with a Translation, an Introduction and a Philosophical
Commentary* (New York: Cambridge University Press,
1982), and Part III.3.46 of Ockham, *Summa logicae*, P.
Boehner, G. Gál, and S. Brown eds. (St. Bonaventure,
NY: Institutum Franciscanum, 1974). Paul Vincent
Spade's *The Medieval Liar: A Catalogue of the
Insolubilia-Literature* (Toronto: Pontifical Institute
of Medieval Studies, 1975) chronicles the develop-
ment of massive interest in the "liar" paradox among
logicians from the 13th to the 15th century.

57 Nicholas Rescher, *Paradoxes: Their Roots, Range, and
Resolution* (Chicago: Open Court, 2001).

58 "The summers of 1903 and 1904 we spent at Churt
and Tilford. I made a practice of wandering about the
common every night from eleven till one ... I was trying
hard to solve the contradictions mentioned above.
Every morning I would sit down before a blank sheet
of paper. Throughout the day, with a brief interval for
lunch, I would stare at the blank sheet. Often when
evening came it was still empty ... the two summers
of 1903 and 1904 remain in my mind as a period of
complete intellectual deadlock. It was clear to me that

Some contemporary books have presented paradoxes as interesting and amusing, like puzzles and riddles. But for the most part, and for most of the history of Western philosophy, paradoxes have been considered an embarrassment, to be avoided at all times, if you wish your argumentation to be considered properly rational. In this respect, philosophers seem to be comparable to theorists in quantum physics, who consistently try to avoid equations with infinities, and who most recently have developed String Theory[59] with that in mind.

But in the meantime, religion and literature, for some reason, seemed to find no particular problem in dealing with apparent contradictions in paradoxes; and these are the paradoxes with which most people are familiar.

In religion, Christians are familiar with Gospel paradoxes—"the first shall be last," "he who loses his life will save it," "it is better to give than to receive," "be simple as children and wise as serpents." But paradoxes are prevalent in other religions also. For example, in the Hindu *Upanishads* we are admon-

---

I could not get on without solving the contradictions, and I was determined that no difficulty should turn me aside from the completion of *Principia Mathematica*, but it seemed quite likely that the whole of the rest of my life might be consumed in looking at that blank sheet of paper."

59 "String theory" in particle physics treats elementary particles as extended one-dimensional "string-like" objects.

ished that "The Spirit is within all, and also outside," and that "Far, far away is [the spirit of Atman], and yet he is very near, resting in the inmost chamber of the heart." The Buddhist *Prajnaparamita Sutras* tell us that "when freed from abiding [with thoughts], you are said to be abiding with the non-abiding." And paradoxes are rampant in the *Tao te Ching* of Chinese religion: for example, "those who know do not talk, and talkers do not know"; or "choosing hardship, the Wise Man never meets with hardship all his life," or "the Wise Man, having given all he had, is then very rich indeed."—This last saying is reminiscent of the Christian paradox that it is "better to give that to receive," and some of the other non-western paradoxes also find parallels in Christianity.

In modern literature, there is almost unanimous agreement that G.K. Chesterton is foremost in the use of paradox in his non-fictional prose works. One finds paradoxes on almost every page. For example, in *Orthodoxy*, Chesterton observes that: "the Christians of the Middle Ages were only at peace about everything (the cosmos)—they were at war about everything else"; and that Christianity combines the love of martyrdom with the hatred of suicide, and the hatred of crime with the love of the criminals.

As regards poetry, a literary theory emerged in the mid-twentieth century, dubbed "The New Criticism," which claimed that paradox was not only important in poetry, but actually constituted the essence of poetry. New Critics, such as Cleanth Brooks, saw paradoxical language as bringing about the reconciliation of opposites, and thus serving as the most striking feature of great poetry. One thinks, for example, of passages such as the following from T.S. Eliot's *Little Gidding*:

> When the short day is brightest, with frost and fire,
> The brief sun flames the ice, on pond and ditches,
> In windless cold that is the heart's heat,
> Reflecting in a watery mirror
> A glare that is blindness in the early afternoon.

The New Criticism has been superseded by other theories. But whether or not one agrees with the New Critics about the identity of poetry and paradox, there is general agreement that the so-called "metaphysical poets," like John Donne and Andrew Marvell, are particularly noteworthy for paradoxes[60]—although not precisely what *I* would call "metaphysical" paradoxes.

Which brings us back to philosophy. Have philosophers ever managed to get beyond their apparent fixation with the "logical paradoxes"? Yes, substantive paradoxes transcending logical paradoxes have been broached here and there, dispersed throughout

---

60 An example from John Donne's *Lecture upon a Shadow*: "For I/ Except you enthrall me, never shall be free,/ nor ever chast, except you ravish me."

the history of philosophy. For example, Heraclitus among the pre-Socratics tells us that the only stable and constant thing in nature is movement and flux; Socrates in Plato's *Apology* claims that his wisdom consists in knowing how much he does not know, and in other Platonic dialogues he leads us to the paradoxical conclusions that we can only know what we already know, that it is better to suffer injustice than to perpetuate it, and that the only person who should be entrusted with kingship is someone who doesn't desire it; the Stoics taught that "only those are free who know that they are not free"; and Hegel, although he was not formally engaged in formulating paradoxes, starts off his *Logic* with the paradox that "being is nothingness" and begins his *Philosophy of Right* with the paradox that "the rational is the real."

Such substantive paradoxes are of great importance. I tend to agree with Roy Sorensen, who compares the importance of paradoxes in philosophy with the significance of prime numbers in mathematics:

> Mathematicians characterize prime numbers as their atoms because all numbers can be analyzed as products of the primes. I regard paradoxes as the atoms of philosophy because

> they constitute the basic points of departure
> for disciplined speculation.[61]

Just as prime numbers are factors in all non-prime
numbers, so also an analysis of the crisscrossing
arguments among philosophers of different persua-
sions will very often yield a paradox at the bottom,
which resists further analysis.

Descartes' complaint about the continual disarray
on the part of philosophers disagreeing on philosophical issues is still valid, although there is also
considerable disagreement that Descartes himself
was able to rise above this. Yes, philosophers dis-
agree on just about everything. And yes, we might
ask, why can't they come to a consensus on basic
principles, as do, for example, the physicists and
chemists, who at least agree on things like gravity
and the periodic table—or as do the mathematicians, whom Descartes praised as the paragons
of certainty and unanimity? The reason for the
endemic philosophic disagreements may be the fact
that philosophers, possibly unconsciously envious
of the scientists and mathematicians, try to imitate
them. They would like very much to come out with
final and straightforward conclusions to philosophical problems, saying definitively, for example, "the
mind is connected to the body through x," or "the

---

61 Roy Sorensen, *A Brief History of the Paradox:
Philosophy and the Labyrinths of the Mind* (Oxford:
Oxford University Press, 2003), p. xi.

precise difference between humans and the other animals is x," or "the ultimate cause of the universe is x." But perhaps it would be worth their while to search out the paradoxes which may be at the roots of some continuing impasses.

The paradoxical conclusion I arrive at is this: *Paradox itself, in literature, religion, and even in philosophy, may be the clearest, and even the simplest, way to express concepts which would have diminished force, and even diminished validity, if expressed in normal assertoric speech modes.* In other words, complexities and oppositions in reality and human life are perhaps best captured by paradoxical language, which, by definition, incorporates the complexities and the oppositions dynamically.

This has been my defense of paradox. The Defense rests, awaiting the Prosecution's cross-examination.

ISBN-13: 978-0-87462-173-0
ISBN-10: 0-87462-173-9

51500

9 780874 621730

www.marquette.edu/mupress/

The Aquinas Lectures
Published by the Marquette University Press
Milwaukee WI 53201-1881 USA
All volumes available as ebooks. See web page:
http://www.mu.edu/mupress/

1. *St. Thomas and the Life of Learning.* John F. McCormick, S.J. (1937) ISBN 0-87462-101-1

2. *St. Thomas and the Gentiles.* Mortimer J. Adler (1938) ISBN 0-87462-102-X

3. *St. Thomas and the Greeks.* Anton C. Pegis (1939) ISBN 0-87462-103-8

4. *The Nature and Functions of Authority.* Yves Simon (1940) ISBN 0-87462-104-6

5. *St. Thomas and Analogy.* Gerald B. Phelan (1941) ISBN 0-87462-105-4

6. *St. Thomas and the Problem of Evil.* Jacques Maritain (1942) ISBN 0-87462-106-2

7. *Humanism and Theology.* Werner Jaeger (1943) ISBN 0-87462-107-0

8. *The Nature and Origins of Scientism.* John Wellmuth (1944) ISBN 0-87462-108-9

9. *Cicero in the Courtroom of St. Thomas Aquinas.* E.K. Rand (1945) ISBN 0-87462-109-7

10. *St. Thomas and Epistemology.* Louis-Marie Regis, O.P. (1946) ISBN 0-87462-110-0

11. *St. Thomas and the Greek Moralists.* Vernon J.Bourke (1947) ISBN 0-87462-111-9

12. *History of Philosophy and Philosophical Education.* Étienne Gilson (1947) ISBN 0-87462-112-7

13. *The Natural Desire for God.* William R.O'Connor (1948) ISBN 0-87462-113-5

62. *Science, Religion and Authority: Lessons from the Galileo Affair.* Richard J. Blackwell. (1998) ISBN 0-87462-165-8

63. *What Sort of Human Nature? Medieval Philosophy and the Systematics of Christology.* Marilyn McCord Adams. (1999) ISBN 0-87462-166-6

64. *On Inoculating Moral Philosophy against God.* John M. Rist. (2000) ISBN 0-87462-167-X.

65. *A Sensible Metaphysical Realism.* William P. Alston (2001) ISBN 0-87462-168-2.

66. *Eschatological Themes in Medieval Jewish Philosophy.* Arthur Hyman. (2002) ISBN 0-87462-169-0

67. *Old Wine in New Skins.* Jorge J. E. Gracia. (2003) ISBN 0-87462-170-4.

68. *The Metamorphoses of Phenomenological Reduction.* Jacques Tamininaux. (2004) ISBN 0-87462-171-2.

69. *Common Sense: A New Look at an Old Philosophical Tradition.* (2005) ISBN-10: 0-87462-172-0; ISBN-13:978-0-87462-172-3.

70. *Five Metaphysical Paradoxes.* Howard P. Kainz. (2006) ISBN: 0-87462-173-9; ISBN-13: 978-0-87462-173-0.

The Aquinas Lectures

About the Aquinas Lecture Series

The Annual St. Thomas Aquinas Lecture Series began at Marquette University in the spring of 1937. Ideal for classroom use, library additions, or private collections, the Aquinas Lecture Series has received international acceptance by scholars, universities, and libraries. Hardbound in maroon cloth with gold stamped covers. Uniform style. Some reprints with soft covers. Complete set (ISBN 0-87462-150-X) receives a 40% discount. New standing orders receive a 30% discount. Regular reprinting keeps all volumes available. Ordering information (purchase orders, checks, and major credit cards accepted):

Marquette University Press
        Phone: (800) 247-6553
        Fax: (419) 281 6883
or order online at: http://www.mu.edu/mupress/

Editorial Address:
Dr. Andrew Tallon, Director
Marquette University Press
P.O. Box 3141
Milwaukee WI 53201-3141
Tel: (414) 288-1564 FAX: (414) 288-7813
email: andrew.tallon@marquette.edu